dedicated to:

those who don't necessarily
find solace in a
single night,

those with diaries ripping
at the seams with
unspoken ideas.

to all those unrequited lovers,
in imagination.

to those people.
the—truly kind, selfless
people who

give knowing no recognition will come,
let those they care for read their face and
answer
when they call.

those alone but, don't find themselves lonely,
for they know the value of the world
and the all-encompassing love that surrounds
it,

to every fleeting hope
each surge of random compassion.

to every person that feels,
human.

SUFFIXES FOR LOVE

By Lou Boltonia

Table of Contents

Introduction.

It is with a great sense of love that I put this book of poems out into the world. The poems here range from some of my earliest writings to ones that date no less than a few months ago, all carefully selected to be a part of this book. This collection has been a long time in the making, as it seems whenever the transitional period between winter and spring arrives, I come back to this. But here it is, the product of many years and much love, from me to you. There are old muses here, ends of eras, and what comes after. It is all I wish for that you find a poem, verse, line—any single thing that says something you haven't yet explained yourself. Or maybe something you've been thinking on forever... expressed just now into words.

—Lou Boltonia

I Only Loved You More.

as sure as East's nam-ed grief

and Westerns' golden peak—

the shores bore a heart-bound thief,

convened from the star-crossed creek.

I've been called twice by my name

by their ego's solid grip—

every tale should be my bane,

if my soul should ever slip.

yet hearth's warmth will spark again

in steel traps with tooth-ed plates,

and twin flames cannot pretend

to be lost of their soulmate-s.

I. THE DARK-LINED SPACE

the point at which December fades

two comes together

blurs of brush, watercolours,

or oil pastels—dipped acrylics

vibrating along the width of a stroke,

enough to singe and

smear thick, melting

away.

part of the scenery.

one

was all it needed to become

two, felt as simple

as humans could. two,

with eyes and hearts as the only witnesses;
no other artists in the room.

one—
was coming from the corners
off gramophones bell, bouncing
low where they stood, rolling
under the bed. notched frames
and pacifying words—
blast it, I was promised
simple.

and two came together.
where slides and clashes
had no differing definitions,
because no one person could tell

the passing of the countryside—
discomfort like

hot grapes
and yellow nights.

in the back of a photo,

honey rain
keeps us where you'd rather not be
pressing face
in need of skin, to comfort
at the most inopportune times.

I could never act the part

of the cigarette-wielding tar-faced smooth-eyed
whimsical driver,
hellbent on treacherous bends

slick by the tempest,

for one.

Honeysweet

a terrible chasm

I had only ever been warned of.

splits the scene,

at the seams,

to confirm its shift.

she had the skin of

whatever you get on the other side

when you filter speckled sun through

honey, on only a very slight tilt.

youth

as a goddess I could only liken

to forever. with dark,

dark *eyes—why they talk as if* brown

is a word unsavoury *I could* never—

not black nor quite burnt, amber.

yet the thinnest line of universal

horizons, where all lights and oceans and

skies, breath of every living thing

converses to fold

the flow *of it all,*

a negative ease.

if only, never,

could've left her

propensity.

but some insignificant beings

never get that second chance,

or even the initial recognition

of that spark.

lest mine,

an unusual one.

surely lit only by

wheat golden, yellow warm, candy-

dipped shades;

that peer from edges

back at me across an unreachable,

unimaginable precipice of an

im-mense schism.

Volatile

cold bones stifle warm hearts—

it's the temperature of

this budding (something) of ours;

chills from spine to hands

smother ember's encore.

I wish I could say the same

for lovers of equal temperature

(lukewarm feelings meet tepid minds)

blinders jammed with forceful screws—

tunnel vision, blissless effect,

(ice spear nails and warped depth perception)

corrosive, decayed,

(fire-fed breaths and impulse surges)

two souls, intervaled calibers,

with no love between them.

Resonance

to the bend of a lip, cupid's position above
me never felt as such a reality. gradients be
damned—it—paper skin could suffer in
the light of this warm olive, not meant to burn
yet leaves careless embers in wake,
single entities,

Lovely, sacred thing; the eyes staring back
in the night are shaded
brown
(barely there), any emerald glint, sapphires
under dark waters; hue in peripheral
or otherwise and I—to be
doomed, a regular Othello.

your resident: who, as halls clacked tile under
the deviant soul, so famed by lit critics as a
soul-eater
took dregs out of the black, cooled
my white felt on fire, pale; warmed—
never a touch between, now or then.
but the coals in your eyes were what
brought my flames less than safe return and

this ocean;
(selfish)
despite any thoughts in your harbour,
was not yours to begin with.

fingers bespoke in form that
are not for a pianist,
long in any way, still wrench my soul

"forget this"

one more selective idea. nothing to repeat or
request of me. left hidden by a dust ruffle
yellowed daisies sparked between
imagined clouds, not too far from their
smoking match head cousins, make
the bed
yet even moral law
could not forsake me this feeling.

please has never been so harsh a whip;
goodbye, never such a salve for the wound.
of doors, empty walls from baby blue
soaked through with
oil-prints, courtesy of the dusk settling us
earlier that evening.

23

almost—a javelin stained in a merciful truth

still stings the skin of the heart wayside that

grinded a ribcage's crushed interior.

closer ever more

in the way ships part in opposite of the wind

rose

yet contain the same brazen compass

bloody-tips drawn together. in

resonance.

By the Line

lose those telling eyes and

the hair is gone.

cut behind my back.

don't let me see—it would

end with where she walked

"what for"

all of it gone,

gone again.

shear to the brim—

sheer to the brim—

to the *edge*,

the brink of losing.

don't let this straw hat (straw man)
glide so smooth around the edges.

and don't we love it.
watching every day without
the someone we
care for.
it brings us to that brink again—
the messy edge that so resides in the
peripheral
to bring us back, or,
lose us again.

once

once is all it takes as
one moment is no ratio for
what defines a decision;

it is an end

to all 3:4,

70:30 that was before

to return is nothing when the brink hovering

deep in a vision is met

and overcome.

it only comes

once

only ever once.

A Necessary Truth

there's a block between me

a space, missing,

love and lust are distant

but the rancor that fuels my righteous, grueling

anger

is closer than ever.

it never leaves.

Hazy Windows in Misty Nighttimes

a gentle numbing hum

    only the sea knocks at my door

akin to a past lover

looking to rekindle flames their waves put out.

(sleep, rest—

both strangers to this new existence

I find myself a part of.)

death is no end,

drowning no sentence.

there is a blackness above,

beyond the sea,

and the crackle of flames

where a gentle numbing hum resonates.

    the lull

i close my eyes and count to ten—

afraid of what I'll see between the flashing

numbers

with my eyes open.

Wound Anew,

a scab begging to heal
(I see my relationships in it)
my teacher is an eagle,
waiting to snatch up our creation
(I wonder how I will learn now)
the scab began to ooze—
in the midst of his talons
the gory details of how I live
macabre even for a wound
and a selfish instructor.

don't keep a hole in your heart,
ready with worry for me

it was by my own hand—

my own intrinsic fault

(only human)

that the old wound of relationships

(flesh, burnt canyons

that are aging black,

liquid curdled gel)

began to bleed again.

II. THE VIEW FROM UP HERE

Bittersixes.

Romance never appealed much to me

but in the light of another's doe-eyed

reflection, their novelistic fantasy,

(from a dream of an angel-born consequence)

the lens flare

burns into me, from them. how they protrude

through word on

fine letter and in some sacred moments, all

romance is

tree sap too light for resin, too sticky a fluid for

beauty and

split apples spilling, disgusting, where they are

unwanted and

blabbering absurdity of the discomfiting kind
making less

sense than what is real, fit for no one, but it is

all that may spark safety—salvation—the one
moment left

for someone that holds them as glue dots on
the tip of the

thread to a future almost lost. yet, come

time, it may also be all that it takes; the final
step from what once was.

glass whims. whistles to the wind.

he looked at others
in the world just as anyone
thinks they must be looked upon
when under someone's utter
devotion.

    a gaze that pins any being
that has space left, boring
frozen pockets where the idea
of fostered connections, would
lay in any sane
being.
(unattainable as a mythical beast,
acquiesced to eternal

slumber.)

even if they know, he

loves each passing person

just as them,

it is a feeling

they will never shake

a loyalty

to.

(not like the

depressive sadness, that stays

and entangles everyday lives.

but the somber, melancholy stasis of

a blanket that doesn't press upon a heavy head

yet wraps around the shoulders,

touted about, taught close on odd days
and loosened to the soil when
suffocating.)

Love Is a Quick One; Love Is a Victim

are you to be the one

who'll pull the tight towers from between my

lips?

loose, they will not protest.

it's safe to say I felt uneasy

when the midmorning sky resembled opal.

where light shed through thinning veils,

through gold and periwinkle;

the solidness of 'above' was suffocating

in the imagined, endless blue and

something open to dream of

a heaven to—

look forward to—

39

steel-lined and pine carvings or

plain oak's sharp corners

caskets are the frankest of vessels.

to the chapel of the garden,

religion is the bend of lily leaves

for when I return,

bulb of the earth,

wax leaves and a yellow trumpet

will sprout my soul anew.

what, you say, a spiderweb.

a conspiracy theory of kindness

that maybe humanity has some inherit

instinct—of ethics, morality,

and its seed was planted in you.

but, forgive me when I say

doubt runs a river at high tide;

glitching—

glitching—

as an analog clock or,

the waves off my back.

a terrible time promised wings

what will for

the town left a memorial for mother's

the ditch for mercy's sister

no deliverance to a grave

shallow trenches are all born from it.

Behind the Building

and the moment was lost.

her kicking the hay as if

the greenhouse hideaway was not enough.

we all know of

sidelong glances, seen them

many a time—nothing strange—

no stranger, to us.

of course

the posture—this Picasso-body language—a dead

giveaway,

I should, we, should have,

known. but the beat came back and

so did I, in that moment.

(yes, just like that)

free-er by-the-by

every day,

a fire starts anew from below the sternum.

and before you know it,

the two are married

joy flitters and flutters around the

"hearts" so tucked away in the minds of

the crowd who believes them to be real and

not eggshell moths clutching tight—precious

space in the shape of folded doves reaching

yet hidden wingtips.

before you know it

the sky-line walls have

come crashing down around that

vanilla feeling.

dear, honeysweet, it's much past time to leave

for every night,

there comes the stomping monster of angst we

tend to as if pretending these meek coals are

still

that flame, filtering auras from deep

within.

the less superficial we wish to be,

Gaia principles

stir this pot of thought, brought to a boil

by others who hold these lines, threads,

yarn and twine in cellars—branching

far beyond and endlessly below the

foggy bridges that

line our lower lids.

they believe (they do not tell) they believe
it is not their own, nor their place.

hold on to that which makes it so,
the threads that fray are not held with
the tightest grip. spared through the
sacrifices of its clustered brothers, equipped
with true want from the beholders;
merely the origin of themselves.

the dark does seep the same as light,
and unity formed the ominous winds
so nearly silent
a mere shave of ice off frosted
leaf-sides would be heard by
the human ear.
beyond her gold-dusted morals and

outstretched

beacon, the mortal does see a finite place;

where from her perch she may only view

eternity,

a Hail Mary of purity.

Camp Song

(1) mere strangers

stumbled by eternal love.
one star, long enough becomes

quietly quivering limbs, the still listeners;
that grab hold of the mindlessly bent lens
thought extinguished
as those long gone were right
and I would be too—

pure, pure

irony—it clouded my thoughts.

(2) a star,

with night bleeding slow indigo, the
same as the lake harbouring
near perfect cooling
gradients to

no end.

I had
fallen. in love.
economics: the pain of
prickling grass,
humid-born bugs flitting on
damp skin
(outweighed;
by the luminous harbour I seek
by the piers

soft woods)

of those

bugs, drowned by our human

nature.

(3) lantern below

a velveteen blackhole

could spin stories—how

the branches were the same and

thousands of lightyears of space entwined,

and everything constituted

the same hues as

our green earths blushing blue-violet lakes.

always of tainted earth

dirt on knees,

under fingernails

weed-pulling: a sacrifice to and of the sun,

but in the dark—insects were

stars and the night was

a lake, with toothed oaks flipped by

force, carving mountainous peaks that could

come

crashing down, with any given second, any

sparing moment

 all was land, up was down; and I

sensed a whole converging.

we were all fickle—

and I loved the indistinction.

(4) believe me—in

the dark

I scribbled over a million pages to a memoir

(or so it felt)

never thinking, might I be misconstrued...

maybe obituaries would be kinder to me.

because I felt it,

feeling. something—

is better than half the chaos we live in.

I hope you will...

forgive my deconstructed nature,

for the love of this

penciled-in exhaustion,

look at the stranger teetering on the

same harsh existence one over

and become to them,

existential.

(5) in this deep expanse

there is no innocence.

take them home to

feel human (small),

let them whisper to you

in night where you would believe it so

truly, neither an innocent, nor a

child,

the moon adjusts the nights' dimmer switch

(it's what they'll say—

stare, ever-moving)

you will always be one with
them.

(6) clouds over the camp.
lake leaves nothing
between
but thin lines,
eyes of house lights
(Gatsby: be jealous)
all shadows on show.

relish in it;

take the beats above and

below into one of your hearts.

it will never leave you

moments pause.

the light kiss of Love

leaves those raptured remains in fragments;

bright wakes for cherry-twinkled dancers.

(two ripples in the pool)

reflections for mirrors bouncing thick love-

fog back in eyes so rose-blown; wide full and

drinking in the distance. alight

with that never before

touched, bestowed upon wreaths of wonder as

millimeter-brush fingertips breech miles

bridging an expansion of

air, warmth, too heavy, no

obstruction of that which dimly burns—

simmer, young flame!

love such as this

alights in tandem with the sun

glimpsing the cut edge of a seabird

wing, not the time it takes for a dew drop

to form on a palmate leaf, but

that it takes to fall.

each spiraled arm in the gold chain takes

no roots to tarnish. hands hatch its length and

intertwine round the necks, parallel.

too brief, to be so silent—

flashbulb reminiscence

reining still, ever delicate.

Gone by the Pull Alone

.

I thought of driving to

Paris, all the way from the

States. just because

the city of romance must be closer to our

moon,

shouldn't it?

and I could

spread my scarf upon the well-traveled winds

before my eyes, grief-stricken as widows

blocking the bridge of lights and

muddied brigade of bricks

where only my telescope of unheard sights

would let flimsy fingers through,

my moon as my lens to my lady, the stars—

a galaxy all the same beneath London-like

smog, this era that so seeks to shroud it in

byproduct.

with l'amour in my throat and wine

warming in my breast,

it would redden my sallow skin;

to see me so calm, in mirth,

surrounded by their warmth—

on fire by love.

.

it is.

I haven't experienced it yet,
maybe I never will.
but that stubborn nature leaving
wistful souls swallowed in the ground,
not deep enough a ditch to be titled
'*grave*'.
greater than the ocean
only to bring blankets and a promise
that same night.

> leftovers forfeited, not a heart broken or a
> second thought.
> something golden in the evening
> a strand, sliver of steely-blue between

morning airlines.
every little train stop and hour stacking on
its brothers to behold a list so full, so vulgar
so, heinous in its texts;
with both the moon *and*
the sun, alive—breathing in it—there. even on a
cloudy day it shines, and in the night,
filaments peek through. because nothing
can be one thing
because, without the other

it is a lost concept on people so drowned.
roses left behind, over dipped—lovely browns,
no
blues or what should be the pink has become
the mottled factory of
red, red, red—

not like the heart and lungs that *does* exist
but as sweetheart candy. filling
an artery or two despite it.

Of course, if I told you that
gore in the form of
heartbreak over mattresses
is not heart-to-hearts under the
brazen *bruised* sunset.
denial would reign strong over
something you claim
unaltered iron—
but if I said
that this *red* is not the passion you
so seek on empty nights
because your mind is meaningless
youth, trapped in a forever.

this red is true passion, as the fruit

showed that the trees gave us, and the real

red that was spilled over front lines between

one heart and an overseas

or whatever so-have-you that brought

some together and apart again

that—

that

is love.

III. THE SOLID, WET EARTH

Ode

Beneath the sycamores,

body gone but love left

I hope you know you are protected.

a thistle sock

set out for the goldfinches

(flocks in the morning, 7:00 a.m.—I counted)

you always loved

better than I.

dappled light,

through their leaves,

never full sun

(but never all shade, either)

I know just the way you liked it.

butterfly bushes

and lilac hyssop; blooms in the fall

now behind white barked saplings.

I hope the sycamores

grow tall in your name—

you always did love better than I.

Mine Eyes, that Wane as the Moon

thoughts come to me,

under the weight of the comforters.

under the weight of a cat and a near-broken air

conditioner,

if I close my eyes now

I won't have to see another person

ever again.

never.

to have roaming stands, pewed as a fish eye

where my own reflection looks back as

blinding as the stage lights,

intimidating as my own opera—sans me.

varnished walls, holy plum, in

broken glass; realigned, reformed, reborn—

would be but a memory and a re-

construction, of a formulaic self.

imagine me—a livewire,

limber with enough wit to perform the

acrobatics up, and away from

what makes me flinch where my stitch-work

has failed me.

It'd only require the sounds of something

horrid...

floorboards snapping

or nail's resistance

feigning. waning.

I would not have one

responsibility, but—

to feel.

Giver

would one rather be
ripe without the tender. a
pomegranate, lovely in juice, spilling
seeds from all sides
behind toughened
flesh.
or maybe tender, forever shy, ripeness bereft
and left wanting.
something to think on. being
soft veal; white, pale, ivory,
pearl that
falls apart on fork but
will never melt in the

mouth, as the sourness of

too early

is more lemon-acid than what

blueberry-soft skins have to

give when

picked at

dusk.

cordless.

.

to construct the veined highway
bleeding through pulp,
a red felt trap on the missing word
would elect the drilling boundaries for a hole,
deep within.
lead-lines, meant for those in good faith,
those coreless marks that so form
a target upon whichever and

whoever they please.
flat mouth faces tell us—
don't live in regrets. "no regrets"
pah! how dull, how nothing and

twice over two-dimensional would
life be then.
not to say; an egret of peace could
steady for landing, and to see
your burdened lead bearings
create comet trails cutting still dusk
as the water fowl was destined to.
velvet cake spills at a young boy's
fifth birthday. stuck in the pores of
defunct foam, around the padded
swings.
but—shoved to the side, is that sweet choice.
never seen, never heard the feather brushes to
call, why, to be
blamed.

even if it's the first air you breathe

the child always has a heart to be moved

so where's where if you can't remember it as

'home'; might as well be

the one that chose you out by

then.

I can't recall if I was on the evens or odds

or if

I was to marry Friday's nimbus—or

Monday's cumulus.

without it we

exist an inch to the left

with

the Harrisburg LED on the dash

counting down when it's

supposed to be up, after

every three-score set of seconds,

every hour.

swung to sleep,

as if the silence of generations never left your

heart

that never went there once in every beat

'tis but a feeling.

the way the two would part

as if it's the same as a breaking

of the continents

.

patchwork remains forever.

roses are hinged behind my eyes
on the brink, looking out instead of in.

they keep popping up in-between these lobes,
this grey-matter

and not in person.

(I'm not as quick to show my allegiances)

Driving does wonders for your nervous system

not exactly

for those threads or, clusters of electrical

wires, electrician's riddle;

but that entanglement of anxious-mess and

wrecked worry

sure will grow.

My words, grown and harvested, in quilts and

in stories,

are patchwork.

But how I love the road

and be it dim foreground lights

or the swath of dust after mist is fried

and trees are sparse to nothing—

my words are patchwork,

when the roses pop up roadside

and not under the cloudy irises

where their seeds,

sheltered,

fell.

Fluid

The forty-five is replaced by the fifty-five,
and it
sucks around the tanned sheet metal like a
warm sleeve. Rain had nothing on us, it
stayed shut under blackened bolts that day.
You said, there in the cigarette butts I hate
and the ash that kept glowing, was an
aesthetic. Something worth looking at.

I seem to remember staring at grey grounds for
quite a while, wondering, where in this
earth were you born to believe something as
this was the epitome of our human dexterity,
how mental time lapse photography of

shattered-out

taillights compared to blurry polaroids

of the Sistine chapel.

Maybe I'll never know.

But theories took to tip-toes in mellowed

circles, rumours behind the ghosted water on

my car windows, because leaving pieces to the

art we have designed to *dismantle* art

that is already *there*—

well why can I not spew up balloons of

words, to fill the room where we sat for

hours in silence, maybe to you a

desperate act to hide sorrowful

faces because we haven't had bad luck

this week just bad experiences,

(we knew we could have rung those strings

criss-cross over the walls every which

way, saved what little we could from

those glib hands—skinning severances, taken

less classes in

nothing, less in general for some

extra sanity—anything to let up

that)

or maybe I'd just rather see the backs of tinfoil

and plastic seams than another glimpse

of pock-marked and marred-to-the-brink skin.

less

ash and asphalt, less glowing temptation for

rotten promises,

I'd (really) like some sunshine, for once

inside these dampened walls of neo-metal and glass.

I say I will never know.
But I never thought you did—would—either.

soft air

my heart hurts,
it constricts with every beat,

burning bonfires in the backyard
settling the wails of fiddles,
double-stops that rise with ash
to speckled stars

every individual muscle
every fiber their own,
hardens, tighter

and the last leaf that couldn't catch
flame. finds imaginary lines in the aura
wrapping about the pile, to join its

sibling's souls, even if they now will never
touch.

half its size,

they strain as if caught and full of

regret

for the dense world that faces it

and the panicked compressions

that keep it

clipped.

the space around me stales

all too quickly.

this chord.

joyous song stuttered in my head

'til rhythm warped and

the air conditioning crept out, a mimic of

angels' static voice

wishing, as if they were never stars that granted

such wonders,

for me to forget—

or, very well, eject these thoughts

guide these lights,

right straight—into the abyss whence they

came.

for discord and tunes are not hand in hand

and by rejection—

a broken union took another step,

hands in the blackened honey pot,

seeing the other side

seeing what was not mine;

what meant to blindside me

granted insight I could never live with.

dulce, they came. light

unto the strings.

small—a child dreams

only a minor chord

amidst with desperation

could disrupt these measures.

never once have I thought of their return.

cathartic.

there was a vision that came to me—
like a dream, or—no,
out of an old movie. where
the air was thick with use
not abandonment, yellow like the
walls. drowsiness crowned to the headmost
point)
and tanned by the days spent in
dusty, choked sunlight.

my skin was hard
but that was what the bath was for,
why your pale arms, slender and

barely weightless around my waist,

lowered me down as if my

fifty pounds over you were nothing.

you're anything but frail;

and the water was near as invisible

as you,

only in sight when moving from

its melancholy places of thought.

my skin was hard,

too much so to love beyond

it, so the bath was drawn.

and the days passed by a time-

lapse camera, haven for natural

storytellers and those with

attention spans from

the mid 1800's.

my skin will be hard for a while,

but to be less so,
was why we used those
sparse, few gallons in the
first place. why the water
turned opaque, fuzzier than my
head or, a moon opal, where

layers shed in flakes and
swaths—where
my skin was a little less hard
and all it meant was that I
could feel the ivory, like prosthetics,
give me gingerly complacent
taps when it's time for tea.
without any words exchanged,

where the air wouldn't keep them,

(from foot to mouth

there's too much in-between to travel)

and they aren't needed.

A Note from the Author

First off—you made it to the end! You
are deserving of my utmost thanks. This book—
being the first I've ever published—means more
to me than I feel I can say (ironic, considering
that it's a collection of poems). All my love
from the past few years has been set in stone
by these words, the cycles of passion that come
when the ties to someone you once loved
begin to fray, and the acceptance afterwards.

I have another set of poems about
regaining lost love through a new relationship,
but with the hundreds of poems I have waiting
to see the light, I'm afraid they might take a

while to reach you. Love is my drive and my end game. It is a choice one must make and it is what I have chosen to live for. Retaining compassion, fostering an innate kindness—that is the most beautiful thing a person can do— even when we relapse into apathy and bitterness, the potential is there in every person. This is what I believe, and so I hope you have felt that same loss, shame, and bitter love through these poems.

So yes, this is not the last you will see of me (unless of course you wish it to be). If you would take the time to let me know how you felt or give my book a rating I'd love to hear it—even if you despised each and every letter!

www.ingramcontent.com/pod-product-compliance
Lightning Source LLC
Chambersburg PA
CBHW020556030426
42337CB00013B/1111